Great African Americans

madam C. J. Walker

self-made millionaire

Revised Edition

Patricia and Fredrick McKissack

Series Consultant
Dr. Russell L. Adams, Chairman
Department of Afro-American Studies, Howard University

Enslow Publishers, Inc.

40 Industrial Road	PO Box 38
Box 398	Aldershot
Berkeley Heights, NJ 07922	Hants GU12 6BP
USA	UK

http://www.enslow.com

To Alfreda Vance

Revised edition of *Madam C. J. Walker: Self-Made Millionaire* © 1992

Library of Congress Cataloging-in-Publication Data

McKissack, Pat, 1944–
    Madam C.J. Walker: self-made millionaire/Patricia and Fredrick McKissack—Rev. ed.
        p. cm. — (Great African Americans)
    Includes index.
    Content: Christmas baby—Moving up the river—The Walker plan—The Walker team—For a good cause—Timeline—Words to know—Learn more about Madam C.J. Walker.
    ISBN 0-7660-1682-X
    Walker, C.J., Madam, 1867–1919—Juvenile literature. 2. Afro-American women executives—Biography—Juvenile literature. 3. Women millionaires—United States—Biography—Juvenile literature. 4. Cosmetics industry—United States—Biography—Juvenile literature. 4. Cosmetics industry—United States—History—Juvenile literature. [1. Walker, C.J., Madam, 1867–1919. 2. Businesswomen. 3. Afro-Americans—Biography. 4. Women—Biography. 5. Cosmetics industry—History.]
    I. McKissack, Fredrick. II. Title. III. Series

    HD9970.5.C672 W356   2001
    338.7′66855′092—dc 21
    [B]
                                                    00-010055

Printed in the United States of America

10 9 8 7 6 5 4 3 2

To Our Readers:
We have done our best to make sure all Internet addresses in this book were active and appropriate when we went to press. However, the author and the publisher have no control over and assume no liability for the material available on those Internet sites or on other Web sites they may link to. Any comments or suggestions can be sent by e-mail to comments@enslow.com or to the address on the back cover.

Every effort has been made to locate all copyright holders of material used in this book.
If any errors or omissions have occurred, corrections will be made in future editions of this book.

Illustration Credits: Library of Congress, pp. 7, 9, 10, 11T, 11B, 14, 15, 20T; Madam C.J. Walker Collection Courtesy of the Indiana Historical Society (detail), pp. 3, 17B, 18, 19, 20B, 21, 23, 26, 27; Madam C.J. Walker Collection, Courtesy of the Indiana Historical Society, pp. 4, 6, 13, 17T, 25; Special Collections and Archives, W.E.B. Du Bois Library, University of Massachusetts Amherst, p. 24; The Byron Collection, Museum of the City of New York, p. 22.

Cover Illustration: The Byron Collection, Museum of the City of New York (detail); Library of Congress; Madam C.J. Walker Collection Courtesy of the Indiana Historical Society (details).

TABLE OF CONTENTS

Madam C. J. Walker
December 23, 1867–May 25, 1919

CHAPTER 1

Christmas Baby

Before the Civil War, Owen and Minerva Breedlove were slaves. They worked in the cotton fields on a large Louisiana plantation. When the war ended in 1865, so did slavery. Millions of African Americans were freed, including the Breedloves and their children, Louvenia, Alexander, James, and Owen Jr.

Freedom was just about all the family had. Owen and Minerva did not have money, jobs, or a home. All they knew how to do was farm. But they had no land.

The Breedloves did what many other slaves did. They became sharecroppers. They rented land from their old master and farmed it. Owen and Minerva worked long, hard hours on their rented farm. Still they stayed poor. Most of what they earned went to pay back the landowner for seeds and food. There was no way to get ahead.

Madam C. J. Walker was born in this cabin on a cotton plantation in Louisiana.

Picking cotton all day long in the hot sun is hard work.

Owen and Minerva Breedlove were going to have another child. Christmas was not far away. There was no money for gifts. Two days before Christmas in 1867, Sarah Breedlove was born. The family called her their Christmas baby. They had high hopes for this child. She was born free!

CHAPTER 2

Moving Up the River

L ife was hard for Sarah and her family. It got even worse. There were many deadly diseases. Her parents got very sick and died. By 1875, Sarah was an orphan.

Seven-year-old Sarah went to live with her married sister. Louvenia took care of her as best she could. But the cotton crops failed year after year. They needed money to live.

Sarah's brother Alex decided to move across the river to Vicksburg, Mississippi. After a while,

Louvenia and her husband and Sarah moved there, too. The two young women took in laundry to make a living. Soon young Sarah married Moses McWilliams so she could "have a home of her own." On June 6, 1885, Sarah's daughter, Lelia, was born. About three years later, Moses died.

Like this woman, Sarah spent hours scrubbing mountains of dirty clothes in a wooden washtub.

Vicksburg was a river town. Sarah watched riverboats float up and down the river night and day. She decided it was time to move on, too. Sarah moved to St. Louis, Missouri, in 1889.

Soon Sarah had a good laundry business there. But she wondered if life would ever be better for her and Lelia.

Sarah worked hard so Lelia could go to school. Lelia was bright and enjoyed reading. Sarah sent her to Knoxville College in Tennessee. Meanwhile, Sarah wasn't happy doing laundry. She wanted to do more with her life.

In 1889, Sarah moved to St. Louis.

In 1904, Sarah went to hear Margaret Murray Washington speak at a meeting of the National Association of Colored Women in St. Louis. Margaret Murray Washington was the wife of Booker T. Washington, the most well known black leader of the time. She gave a great speech about the rewards of hard work.

Sarah made up her mind. She was going to improve her life.

After hearing a speech given by Margaret Murray Washington, left, Sarah decided to change her life.

Booker T. Washington, the famous African-American leader.

CHAPTER 3

The Walker Plan

there were not many products for black women's hair problems. Sarah's hair was thin and dry. Some of it was falling out. So Sarah decided to make a hair grower to use on her own hair. It worked. Her hair grew longer and thicker.

Lelia was away at college. Sarah had married again, but she divorced her husband. There was nothing keeping Sarah in St. Louis. So she moved to Denver, where her brother Owen's wife and four daughters lived.

Sarah got a job in a drugstore. At night she worked on her hair products. Soon, Sarah began selling her goods from door to door. Black women were happy to have something that made their hair look nice. Sarah's sales were so good, she hired women to help sell door-to-door, too.

This ad showed Madam Walker herself—before and after using her hair care products. Her husband, C.J., helped with advertising.

BEFORE USING

Madam Walker around 1909.

Madame Walker Giving a Manicure

Madam Walker trained women to have a "complete" look: well-groomed hair, well-pressed and clean clothing, and manicured nails.

Sarah had known Charles Joseph (C. J.) Walker back in St. Louis. Now he lived in Denver, too. Their friendship grew into love. On January 4, 1906, Charles and Sarah were married. From that time on, she called herself Madam C. J. Walker.

CHAPTER 4

The Walker Team

When Lelia graduated from college, she came to help her mother. In 1908, Madam Walker and her daughter opened Lelia College in Pittsburgh, Pennsylvania. They trained women in the Walker hair care plan. Women who graduated from Madam Walker's school were called hair culturists.

First the culturist washed the woman's hair. Madam Walker's hair grower was added. Then the customer's hair was pressed with a hot comb and curled.

In 1910, Madam Walker decided to build her first factory in Indianapolis, Indiana. Right away Madam Walker hired people to help build a strong business. Two lawyers, Robert Lee Brokenburr and Freeman Briley Ransom, managed the company.

Violet Davis Reynolds was Madam Walker's secretary and good friend. They traveled together. They showed other black women that they could start businesses, too.

Madam Walker owned several of the latest cars, such as this Model T Ford.

17

The
Walker
company also made
many creams,
powders, and
soaps.

Black women loved the idea! In 1910, most black women made from $2 to $10 a week. Madam Walker's hair culturists were making $20 a week or more.

A year after moving to Indianapolis, the company had 950 salespeople. The company earned $1,000 a month. Madam Walker put the money back into the business. By 1918, her company was earning about $250,000 a year. Madam Walker made history by becoming America's first female self-made millionaire—white or black!

Madam Walker's daughter, A'Lelia.

19

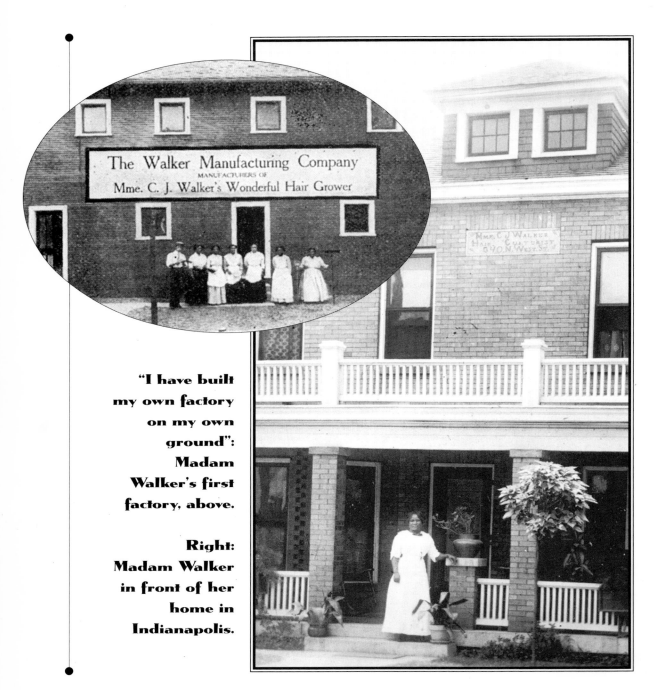

"I have built my own factory on my own ground": Madam Walker's first factory, above.

Right: Madam Walker in front of her home in Indianapolis.

CHAPTER 5

For a Good Cause

Lelia married and changed her first name to A'Lelia. The marriage ended, but she kept the name A'Lelia Walker Robinson. A'Lelia didn't have any children of her own. So she adopted Mae Bryant, a young girl who worked at the Walker factory. Mae had long, thick hair. She became the model for the Walker Company.

Madam Walker used her money to make life better for her family and the people who worked for

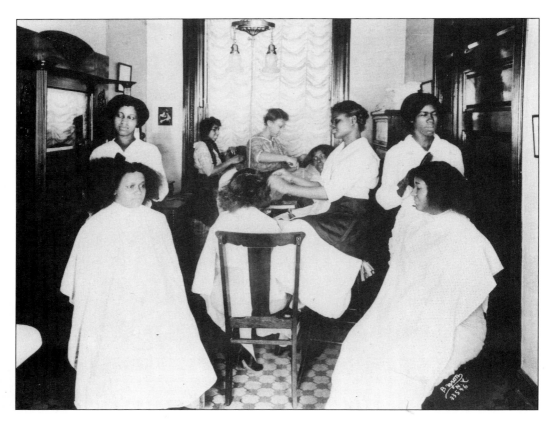

At Lelia College, A'Lelia Walker, seated left, has a scalp treatment. Her daughter, Mae, in back with braids, treats a customer.

her. She also gave freely to churches, schools, hospitals, children's homes, and other good causes.

Madam Walker and A'Lelia were always interested in civil rights. At that time the country was segregated. This meant that laws kept black people and white people apart. Blacks and whites couldn't ride buses or trains together. They couldn't go to the same schools.

Once Madam Walker went to a white theater. They charged her more money because she was black. First she sued the theater. Then she built the Walker Building, a block-long business center in downtown

Madam Walker donated money for Indianapolis's new black YMCA. Next to her is Booker T. Washington. Behind her is F. B. Ransom.

Madam Walker helped organize a parade in 1917 to protest violence against African Americans.

Indianapolis. Inside, there was a new movie theater where black and white people could sit together.

Most jobs weren't open to blacks. Madam Walker spoke to groups all over the country. She believed black people needed to start more businesses in their own neighborhoods. Then there would be more jobs for other African Americans.

In 1913, A'Lelia moved to Harlem, a mostly black neighborhood in New York City. She wanted her mother to move the business there. Harlem was becoming the center of black life.

Finally Madam Walker agreed that New York was the place to live. In 1916, she left Indianapolis.

But the Walker Factory stayed there. F. B. Ransom and Alice Kelly were left in charge. Alice Kelly knew Madam Walker's secret formula. Madam Walker and A'Lelia were the only other people who knew the formula at that time.

Madam Walker had worked hard all her life. Now her health was poor.

Walker agents gather at Villa Lewaro, her mansion overlooking the Hudson River in New York.

Her doctors warned her to slow down, but she did not know how to rest. Madam Walker traveled around the country giving speeches and opening new beauty shops.

Walker in a quiet moment in her New York mansion.

Sarah Breedlove Walker, known as Madam C. J. Walker, died on May 25, 1919. She was fifty-one years old. A'Lelia stayed in New York. She used her great wealth to help struggling black authors, artists, and musicians in the 1920s. In 1931, she died at age forty-six.

26

Madam Walker hoped to inspire other African Americans. With hard work, she became one of the richest women in the United States—black or white.

timeLINe

1867 ~ Sarah Breedlove is born December 23 in Delta, Louisiana.

 1878

1875 ~ Sarah is orphaned.

1878 –1905 ~ Works as a laundress, washing clothes for other people.

1882 ~ Marries Moses McWilliams.

1885 ~ Daughter Lelia is born.

1889 ~ Moves to St. Louis, Missouri; begins making hair care products.

1910

1905 ~ Moves to Denver, Colorado, to start her business.

1906 ~ Marries Charles Joseph (C. J.) Walker and calls herself Madam C. J. Walker.

1908 ~ Opens Lelia College in Pittsburgh, Pennsylvania, to train other women to use and sell her hair products.

1910 ~ Builds factory in Indianapolis, Indiana; begins to work for civil rights for African Americans.

1916 ~ Moves to New York; continues giving much of her money to charities.

1919 ~ Dies on May 25.

WORDS TO KNOW

civil rights—The rights of a free people, including the right to vote.

civil war—A war fought within one country. In the United States, the Civil War was fought between northern and southern states.

factory—A place where products to be sold are made. Madam Walker made her hair products at home until she built a factory in 1910.

graduate—To finish the required course of study at a school.

hair grower—A product of the Walker Company that relieved dandruff and other hair scalp disease. It helped the scalp so hair could grow, but it could not cure baldness.

Harlem—A mostly black neighborhood in New York City. In 1913, only a few black people were living in Harlem. Large numbers of African Americans moved to Harlem after World War I.

National Association of Colored Women (NACW)—In 1896, several national groups of black women joined together under this name. They worked for equal rights for African Americans and women.

WORDS TO KNOW

orphan—A child whose parents are both dead.

plantation—A large farm with hundreds of people who worked in the fields. Before 1863, southern plantations used slaves, like Sarah's parents, to raise cotton and other crops.

secretary—A person who helps in the day-to-day work of a business or an individual.

segregated—Separated from, apart. At one time, the United States had separate schools for blacks and whites. The two races could not work together or share public facilities, like hotels, restaurants, restrooms, and so on.

self-made millionaire—Madam Walker was the first black woman to become very wealthy by earning money through her own business.

slaves—People who are owned by other people and forced to work without pay.

Learn more about Madam C. J. Walker

Books

Colman, Penny. *Madam C. J. Walker: Building a Business Empire*. Brookfield, Conn.: Millbrook Press, 1994.

Lasky, Kathryn. *Vision of Beauty: The Story of Sara Breedlove Walker*. Cambridge, Mass.: Candlewick Press, 2000.

Toby, Marlene and Carol Greene. *Madam C. J. Walker: Pioneer Black Businesswoman*. Danbury, Conn.: Children's Press, 1995.

Internet Addresses

Madame C. J. Walker
<http://www.princeton.edu/~mcbrown/display/walker.html>

Madam C. J. Walker
Web site of A'Lelia Perry Bundles, the great-great-granddaughter of Madam C. J. Walker.
<http://www.madamcjwalker.com>

Madam C. J. Walker
<http://www.indianahistory.org/heritage/madam.html>

index